Extreme
BMX

Weigl Publishers Inc.

Published by Weigl Publishers Inc.
350 5th Avenue, Suite 3304, PMB 6G
New York, NY 10118-0069

Website: www.weigl.com

All of the Internet URLs given in the book were valid at the time of publication. However, due to the dynamic nature of the Internet, some addresses may have changed, or sites may have ceased to exist since publication. While the author and publisher regret any inconvenience this may cause readers, no responsibility for any such changes can be accepted by either the author or the publisher.

Library of Congress Cataloging-in-Publication Data available upon request.
Fax 1-866-44-WEIGL for the attention of the Publishing Records department.

ISBN 978-1-59036-910-4 (hard cover)
ISBN 978-1-59036-911-1 (soft cover)

Printed in the United States of America
1 2 3 4 5 6 7 8 9 0 12 11 10 09 08

Weigl would like to acknowledge Getty Images as one of its primary photo suppliers for this title.

Every reasonable effort has been made to trace ownership and to obtain permission to reprint copyright material. The publishers would be pleased to have any errors or omissions brought to their attention so that they may be corrected in subsequent printings.

EDITOR: Heather C. Hudak
DESIGN: Terry Paulhus
LAYOUT: Kathryn Livingstone

Extreme BMX

CONTENTS

WHAT ARE THE X GAMES?

The X Games are an annual sports tournament that showcases the best athletes in the extreme sports world. Extreme sports are performed at high speeds. Participants must wear special equipment to help protect them from injury. Only athletes who spend years training should take part in these sports. There are many competitions, such as the X Games, that celebrate the skill, dedication, and determination of the athletes, as well as the challenge and difficulty of the sports.

The X Games began as the Extreme Games in 1995. The following year, the name was shortened to X Games. In 1995 and 1996, the games were held in the summer, and they featured a wide variety of sports. These included skateboarding, inline skating, BMX, street luge, sky surfing, and rock climbing.

The popularity of the X Games made it possible for more sports to be showcased. In 1997, the Winter X Games began. The Winter X Games feature sports such as snowboarding, skiing, and snowmobiling. Today, there are Summer and Winter X Games each year.

Some of the best BMX riders in the world compete in the X Games. These athletes perform extreme moves in front of large crowds. Events feature riders performing stunts or racing to the finish line.

TECHNOLINK

Learn more about the X Games at **expn.go.com**.

X FEST

The X Games are about more than sports. Each year, musical acts from all over the world perform for fans at the X Games. X Fest is the name for the musical portion of the X Games. It features some of the best-known punk rock, hip hop, and alternative music artists of the time. These artists perform between sporting events and keep the crowds entertained and excited for the competitions.

WHAT IS BMX?

BMX, or bicycle moto X, is a sport that requires skill, determination, and focus. Athletes ride on specially designed bicycles that have large wheels, usually about 18 to 24 inches (46 to 61 centimeters) wide.

There are several styles of BMX riding. In BMX racing, riders speed along dirt tracks. The first one to the finish line wins the race. In freestyle BMX, riders perform tricks on the bikes.

Over time, five types of freestyle BMX have developed. These are Street, Park, Vert, Dirt, and Flatland. Each type uses the bike in different ways and takes place on various types of **terrain**.

Timeline

1963 – Schwinn develops the stingray. Young people use it to perform tricks.

1970 – One of the founders of BMX, Scot Breithaupt, begins holding BMX races in Long Beach, California.

1974 – The first BMX bike magazine, *Bicycle Motocross News*, is published.

1977 – The American Bicycle Association (ABA) is founded to create standards for BMX racing and tricks.

1978 – BMX is introduced in Europe.

1981 – The International BMX Federation is founded.

In the 1960s, lowrider cars had become popular in parts of the United States. Many young people who could not yet drive or did not have the money to buy a car began to alter their bikes to ride low to the ground, like these cars. Schwinn, a bike manufacturing company, caught word of this trend. In 1963, Schwinn began selling a bike called the stingray. It was smaller than regular bikes and had tall handlebars and a long banana seat that sat low to the ground. Soon, riders were using the bikes to do wheelies, jumps, and other tricks.

In 2008, BMX racing became an Olympic sport.

By the 1970s, California kids were using stingrays to copy **moto X** tricks. Filmmaker Bruce Brown caught the action on camera in a movie called *On Any Sunday*, and people across the nation began using their bikes in a new way. By the mid-1970s, bike manufacturers were designing special bicycles for doing tricks. This was the beginning of BMX.

1982 – The first BMX world championships take place.

1984 – Freestyle BMX becomes an official sport when Bob Morales forms the American Freestyle Association.

1995 – The first BMX events are held at the first X Games.

2002 – At the X Games, Mat Hoffman sets a record by being the first rider to land a no-handed 900, a trick in which the rider jumps off a ramp and spins in the air without holding onto the bike's handlebars.

2003 – The International Olympic Committee (IOC) decides to include BMX in the 2008 Olympic Games in Beijing, China.

ALL THE RIGHT EQUIPMENT

There is no standard uniform for BMX athletes. Freestyle riders often wear loose-fitting T-shirts that allow more movement when performing tricks. Riders also wear long pants, such as jeans, that fit well so they do not get caught on the bicycle when doing a trick. Riders wear shoes with a flat rubber sole that offers better grip on the bike pedals. BMX racers need to protect their skin from rocks and dirt that can fly through the air as they ride at high speeds. They wear pants, long-sleeved shirts, and closed-toe shoes. All riders wear special gloves that allow them to grip the handlebars better.

BMX is an action sport that can be dangerous. A big part of participation is preparation. Even the best riders in the world fall, so when starting out, riders must be prepared to take their fair share of falls. BMX riding often is done on hard surfaces, such as wood ramps, asphalt, and concrete. Riders must wear the proper equipment to protect themselves if they fall.

ACCESSORIZE IT !

Most bikes have 20-inch (51-cm) wheels. Racing bikes have knobby tires. This means that they have a great deal of **tread** to help grip the dirt track and allow for extra speed. Freestyle bikes have a smooth tread for riding on concrete.

The helmet is the most important piece of safety equipment. When falling off a BMX bike, a rider's head can hit the ground. Helmets have saved many riders from serious head injuries.

To take part in BMX, riders need a special type of bicycle. Racing bikes are usually made from lightweight aluminum. They are meant for riding on dirt tracks. Freestyle bikes weigh twice as much as racing bikes. These bikes need to withstand the pressures of tricks and stunts.

Many riders wear knee and elbow pads. These protect elbows and knees as well as other body parts. Riders learn how to use these pads as cushions if they fall.

Some freestyle bikes have pegs on the wheel axles. Riders use these to balance on while performing different tricks.

SURVEYING THE VENUE

B MX riding can be done almost anywhere there is concrete, pavement, dirt, or wood. Skateparks, dirt trails, and vacant lots are perfect places for riders to practice their moves.

Many freestyle BMX riders practice at skateparks. Here, there are obstacles that they can use to perform tricks. One of the main obstacles is a halfpipe. Halfpipes are made from two **concave** ramps, or quarterpipes, that face each other at their lowest points. There is a space between the two ramps. Rather than ride bikes, flatland riders remain in one place as they balance, twist, and spin their bodies around the bike. Flatland riders practice their skill on smooth surfaces, such as paved parking lots or sports courts. BMX racers ride on dirt tracks that have obstacles, such as jumps and **berms**.

At the X Games, there are three BMX events. Each takes place on a different course. The Vert competition takes place on a halfpipe that launches riders high in the air. In Park, competitors use a variety of obstacles, such as **spines**, concrete barriers, and quarterpipes, to perform tricks. The Big Air event includes an 80-foot (24-m) megaramp, quarterpipes, and gaps.

Dirt hills and rough roads are great places to practice BMX riding in nature.

TECHNOLINK

To find out how to build a BMX track, visit **www.prm.nau.edu/ prm423/bmx_track.htm**.

BIG AIR

Big Air at the X Games is an exciting event that has riders facing a series of ramps, pipes, walls, and gaps.

Riders start by taking an elevator ride to the top of a megaramp, which features an 80-foot (24-m) drop. Riders roll down the drop and launch off a quarterpipe at the other end. Then, they soar through the air, performing a single stunt across a gap that spreads up to 70 feet (21 m) wide. They land briefly at the top of another ramp. Without pause, riders roll down that ramp, speeding to the top of another quarterpipe. When they reach the final quarterpipe, riders perform a trick at the top before turning around.

Kevin Robinson took home the gold in the Big Air Finals at X Games 12.

Nine riders take part in this competition. Each rider gets four tries to show his skills to the judges. The judges score the riders based on tricks performed over the gaps and on the final quarterpipe. Each rider's highest score is compared to the others at the end of the selection session. The three top-scoring riders move on to the final round to compete against the winners from the previous year. During the finals, each rider has five runs. Again, the top scores are compared, and the rider with the most points wins the event.

During X Games 12, the Big Air competition took place at Home Depot Center in Los Angeles, California.

BIG AIR PAST WINNERS

2007
Gold – Kevin Robinson
Silver – Steve McCann
Bronze – Anthony Napolitan

VERT

During the Vert, or Vertical, event, 20 of the world's top riders take turns performing their best stunts as they ride along the halfpipe. At X Games 13, the halfpipe stood 153-feet (47-m) wide and 11-feet (3-m) high, with 2 feet (0.6 m) of vertical extensions at the top.

Vert riders ride up one wall of the halfpipe, soar over the top, and perform a trick in the air before landing on the same side of the pipe. From there, they roll down the pipe and up the other wall, performing another trick before landing. In some cases, riders may choose to do a trick on the flat platform, or deck, at the top of each wall. These are called lip tricks. The process of riding back and forth across the pipes is repeated several times before the end of the rider's run.

Jamie Bestwick took home the silver in Vert at X Games 12 in 2006.

Each rider gets two 60-second runs to impress the judges with his skills. Judges look for riders who use the course well, show creativity and style, and get good **amplitude**. The highest score of each rider is compared at the end of the competition. The rider with the most points wins the event.

VERT PAST WINNERS

2007
Gold – Jamie Bestwick
Silver – Simon Tabron
Bronze – Kevin Robinson

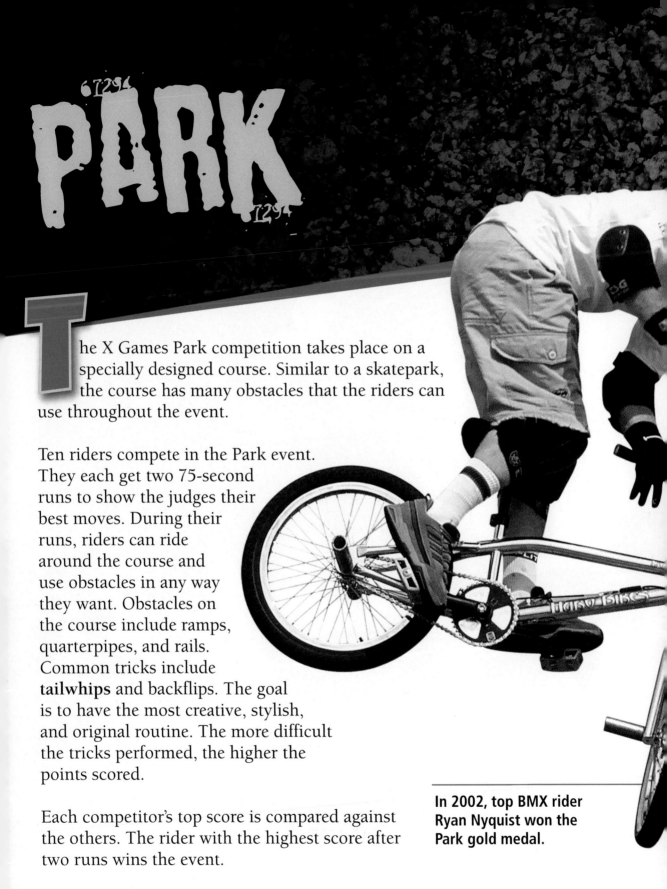

PARK

The X Games Park competition takes place on a specially designed course. Similar to a skatepark, the course has many obstacles that the riders can use throughout the event.

Ten riders compete in the Park event. They each get two 75-second runs to show the judges their best moves. During their runs, riders can ride around the course and use obstacles in any way they want. Obstacles on the course include ramps, quarterpipes, and rails. Common tricks include **tailwhips** and backflips. The goal is to have the most creative, stylish, and original routine. The more difficult the tricks performed, the higher the points scored.

Each competitor's top score is compared against the others. The rider with the highest score after two runs wins the event.

In 2002, top BMX rider Ryan Nyquist won the Park gold medal.

Scotty Cranmer won the gold medal in Park at the 2006 X Games.

PARK PAST WINNERS

2007
Gold – Daniel Dhers
Silver – Scotty Cranmer
Bronze – Dave Mirra

QUALIFYING TO COMPETE

The first step to becoming a professional BMX rider is to get sponsored. Companies sponsor riders by paying them to wear their brand name or logo at competitions or in TV and magazine advertisements selling the company's product. X Games athletes do not need a sponsor to take part in the games, but they do need money to pay for equipment, travel to sporting events, and living expenses while they are training. To become sponsored, a person must be very good at BMX. Riders who perform never-before-seen tricks and push themselves to try new stunts are more likely to get noticed.

TECHNOLINK

To learn how to ride BMX, check out **www.sportskool.com/ videos/intro-to-bmx**.

Sometimes, companies will approach athletes about sponsorship. However, most companies will not know about a good rider unless that person is competing at big events. For this reason, many riders contact companies about sponsorship.

To qualify for the X Games, riders must work hard, practice new tricks, and take part in many events. Each year, 40 of the best BMX riders, as well as up to 10 BMX industry representatives, are asked to nominate riders for the X Games. To place their nominations, they must log in to a secure website to cast their ballot. Each person gets only one vote. The X Games BMX Invitation Committee reviews these nominations to decide which riders should be invited to take part in the games. Top-scoring athletes at recent competitions often receive invitations. However, riders who have a great deal of experience in the sport or who have been featured in many magazines and videos may also be invited to the games.

W hile BMX riding is a unique sport that is popular around the world, it is not the only sport in which the athlete rides a bike. These sports are similar to BMX riding.

Moto X

Moto X, or motocross, riders use specially designed motorcycles to race along tracks or perform tricks and stunts. Most moto X races take place on dirt tracks that have a series of winding turns and muddy hills. Riders race to the finish line as they speed around the track. In freestyle moto X, riders use ramps and other obstacles to perform tricks, such as backflips. Moto X can be done any place where off-road vehicles are able to ride. These often include large fields that have natural dirt ramps and obstacles, such as trees or mud puddles.

Cycling

Cycling is the oldest bicycle sport. This sport can be done in teams or as single-person riders. Cyclists compete in races on closed courses in different pars of the world. Cyclists can reach speeds of more than 70 miles (113 kilometers) per hour. The Tour de France is the biggest international cycling event. The Olympics also include cycling competitions.

Mountain Biking

In mountain biking, athletes ride specially designed bikes over bumpy, rocky trails. Some mountain bikes are lower to the ground than regular bikes. This makes them more steady, and the rider is less likely to fall. These bikes have wide tires that grip the ground better than thin tires.

Ice Biking

In ice biking, cyclists challenge their skills by riding on black ice and packed snow. Like regular cycling, ice biking can be done on paved roads or natural trails. On icy roadways, ice bikers may use studded tires to help grip the slippery path. Often, riding in these conditions requires greater effort, making for a tough workout.

UNFORGETTABLE MOMENTS

Throughout the history of the X Games, there have been many unforgettable moments. These include record-breaking wins, long falls, and new tricks.

At the 2002 X Games in Los Angeles, Mat Hoffman, also known as the Condor, made history during the Vert competition. Hoffman, who had come out of retirement to take part in the event, made sure people took notice. Riders and fans watched anxiously as Hoffman prepared to perform the first-ever no-handed 900. The stunt involves spinning two-and-a-half times in the air before landing. Hoffman successfully completed the trick. However, problems with his handlebars cost him the win. He took home the silver medal instead.

In 2007, Jamie Bestwick took home a gold medal after treating the crowd to a series of well-performed tricks. During his first run, Bestwick tackled a number of difficult stunts, including an opposite flair and a one-footed opposite double flair. These stunts are a variation of the flair, which is a backflip and half-twist in the air. Then, after doing a whip, Bestwick did an opposite double-tailwhip. This was the first time the trick was landed successfully in competition.

During the same competition, Simon Tabron also broke a record by being the first person to land two back-to-back 900s. This secured Tabron the silver medal win.

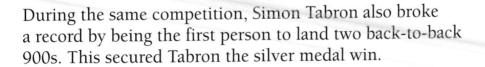

AROUND THE WORLD

Colwood, Canada

Colwood, located southwest of Victoria, British Columbia, has a BMX bike track that is suited to many skill levels. Champion riders have used the track to train for events.

ATLANTIC OCEAN

Columbus, Ohio

The Flow Skatepark is an indoor facility that boasts about 50,000 square feet (4.645 sq km) of riding space.

PACIFIC OCEAN

Chandler, Arizona

The Chandler Bike Park features 25,000 square feet (2,323 square meters) of concrete obstacles, such as ramps, jumps, quarterpipes, and boxes. It is designed specifically for Freestyle BMX riders.

1. Rhode Island, United States
2. Los Angeles, United States
3. Mexico City, Mexico
4. Rio de Janeiro, Brazil
5. Kuala Lumpur, Malaysia
6. Shanghai, China

ARCTIC OCEAN

ARCTIC OCEAN

Shanghai, China

SMP Skate Park the world's largest skatepark. With more than 147,466 square feet (13,700 sq m) of space for riding, some of the world's best BMX riders practice at this park.

Bromley Heath, Great Britain

The skate park in Bromley Heath features many obstacles, including a quarterpipe, ramps, and jumps.

6

PACIFIC OCEAN

5

INDIAN OCEAN

Beenleigh Bike Park, Australia

Located between Brisbane and the Gold Coast, Beenleigh features a variety of ramps and halfpipes designed for BMX riding.

CURRENT STARS

ANTHONY NAPOLITAN

HOMETOWN
Youngstown, Ohio

BORN
March 22, 1986

NOTES
In 2006, won the first stop of the **AST Dew Tour** in Louisville

Performs front flip no-handers and double tailwhip 360s

Nominated for the NORA cup, the most prestigious BMX industry award

DANIEL DHERS

HOMETOWN
Caracas, Venezuela

BORN
March 25, 1985

NOTES
The only rider to frontflip over a spine in competition

Learned how to ride a bike at age 12

Attended Camp Woodward, an action sports camp, in 2004 and 2005

CHAD KAGY

HOMETOWN
Gilroy, California

BORN
November 21, 1978

NOTES
The second person to land a double backflip in competition

Has a scholarship fund that pays the fees for several children to attend Camp Woodward each year

In 2004, broke his neck during practice at the Gravity Games

COREY BOHAN

HOMETOWN
Brisbane, Australia

BORN
January 15, 1982

NOTES
Surfs and spends time with his family when he is not riding

Lives in Corona, California, when in the United States

Finished second place in the 2003 X Games Bike Stunt Dirt Competition

LEGENDS

RYAN NYQUIST

HOMETOWN
Los Gatos, California

BORN
March 6, 1979

NOTES
Appearance as himself on the cartoon *Kim Possible*

Has won 13 X Games medals

Has been featured on the MTV show *Cribs*

MAT HOFFMAN

HOMETOWN
Edmond, Oklahoma

BORN
January 9, 1972

NOTES
Owner of Hoffman Bikes Manufacturing in Oklahoma

Published an autobiography called *Ride of My Life*

In 2005, was elected the president of the International BMX Freestyle Federation

JAMIE BESTWICK

HOMETOWN
Nottingham, UK

BORN
June 8, 1971

NOTES
Signature trick is the downside tailwhip flair

Is a published photographer, with photos appearing in numerous BMX magazines

Is said to be one of the world's best Vert riders

DAVE MIRRA

HOMETOWN
Chittenango, New York

BORN
April 4, 1974

NOTES
Has more X Games medals than any other athlete in history

Is featured in the *Dave Mirra Freestyle BMX* video game series

Has won medals at every X Games since the first one in 1995

THE 10 QUESTION QUIZ

1 In what year were the first X Games held?

2 Where were the first BMX races held?

3 How long is the drop from the top of the megaramp in the Big Air event?

4 What is the most important piece of safety equipment for a rider?

5 How many riders compete in the Park event?

6 Which BMX rider has received the most X Games medals?

7 What are the five types of BMX riding?

8 How long are the runs in the Vert competition?

9 What is Mat Hoffman's nickname?

10 Who built the stingray bicycle?

Answers: 1. 1995 2. Providence & Newport, Rhode Island 3. 80 feet (24 m) 4. A helmet 5. 10 6. Dave Mirra 7. Street, Park, Vert, Dirt, and Flatland 8. 60 seconds 9. The Condor 10. Schwinn

www.fatbmx.com

www.expn.go.com/BMX

www.vitalbmx.com

www.bmxonline.com

Many books and websites provide information on BMX. To learn more, borrow books from the library, or surf the Internet.

Most libraries have computers that connect to a database for researching information. If you input a keyword, you will be provided with a list of books in the library that contain information on that topic. Non-fiction books are arranged numerically, using their call number. Fiction books are organized alphabetically by the author's last name.

GLOSSARY INDEX

amplitude: to be very large

AST Dew Tour: an extreme sports tour that takes place between June and October each year; athletes with the most points in their sport at the end of the tour win top honors

berms: flat strips of land that are raised and border along roads or bodies of water

concave: curved inward

moto X: a sport in which specially designed motorcycles are raced on dirt and concrete tracks or used to perform tricks

spines: ramps that are made from two launch ramps that are placed back-to-back with a small deck between them

tailwhips: tricks done when the back end of the bike spins all the way around while the front end remains in one place

terrain: a piece of land and its natural features

tread: the knobby rubber on a tire